GODLY FINANCES

and
The Bible Way
To Pay Off Your Home

by

DAVID CRANK

Special Dedication

• To my Heavenly Father Who never lost faith in me when so many did.

• To my mother, Maxine Crank, whom I love, but now a resident of that Celestial City.

• To Harold and Karen Black whose middle name is "Faithful to Service."

• To my lovely wife, Sharon, "Joy of My Life."

• To Jesus Who knows me and still loves me.

From The Author

Sharon and I knew people were hurting, but until we started broadcasting television on July 14, 1984, via satellite across the country, I didn't realize how many people were hurting. Letters began to pour into our ministry offices in St. Louis, Missouri, from the East Coast to the West Coast. We read each letter and literally wept because of the needs. We allowed the compassion to flow and to carry us over into intercession and groanings of the Spirit. We believe the direction came to share, by the miracle of the printed page, the truth of God's Word, because Jesus has paid the price for it.

Sharon and I have given our lives to come against one of the forces of hell . . . which is poverty, at all levels, spiritually, mentally, physically, and materially. A wise man once said, "It does no good to curse the darkness, but light a candle." We trust this work to be one of our candles and go from Glory to Glory with this Good News.

David Crank

FOREWORD

Thousands upon thousands of letters arrive each week at our ministry. Some contain the account of a glorious miracle that has taken place, and share how lives have been touched and transformed by God's healing power. A great portion of the mail also contains prayer requests for a variety of needs. Since this ministry is regarded as a healing ministry, I assumed that the majority of the prayer requests received would relate directly or indirectly to prayer for physical needs of healing and deliverance from bondage.

With such a large volume of mail arriving each week, I am not able to read every letter to determine what the people are saying and what needs are on their hearts. That is why I recently asked the individual who supervises our mail to provide a breakdown of the mail for me, outlining the three main types of prayer requests. I wanted to know if there was a common theme, and if so, I could address these areas on our daily television program, "This Is Your Day!"

I was rather surprised at the results of the inquiry. A much larger number of prayer requests than I expected were for financial needs. In addition, a significant amount of letters and telephone calls also requested prayer for family relations and for healing.

God's Promises For Blessing

The Word of God has much to say about the blessings promised to those who love God and walk in His ways. The Bible is filled with many wonderful promises of blessing for God's children, and these promises pertain to every area of life.

The Bible says that "God is not a respecter of persons."

Therefore, the promises contained in God's Word are available to you. You can experience God's blessings in every area of your life. But to experience God's blessings, you must know what His Word promises.

So many believers are missing out on the life of blessing that our loving heavenly Father longs to bestow upon His children. A recent poll in U. S. *News & World Report* reported on the relative happiness of Americans with various aspects of their lives. On a scale 1 through 10, with 1 being lowest and 10 being highest, Americans gave their happiness with their financial situation a score of 5.98. Any score lower than 7 was deemed to denote "relative unhappiness."[1] This is not what God intended for you and me.

You can experience freedom from financial bondage, and know what it is to know "no lack". God's Word offers many promises which deal with "sufficiency in all things". "All things" includes your finances!

Godly Finances is a wonderful book which I discovered in the mid 1980's. From the first time I read this book, it was a blessing to me for its pages contain great wisdom along with truth from God's Word. Not only has this book been a source of blessing to me personally, but it has also proven to be a tremendous help whenever I have taught on this topic from my pulpit.

I am confident that God is more eager to bless us than we are to receive that blessing. So many scriptures in the Bible record the promises of God and His desire to bless us.

I have experienced the reality of God's blessings in the area of my finances. And it's glorious to be free from financial debt and bondage and begin to know what it is to have "no lack".

Godly Finances presents a very balanced message and practical principles which you can begin applying today . . . principles which will help to bring you out of financial bondage! This book also offers a first-hand perspective about finances because it represents the principles which the author, David Crank, has applied to his own life to bring about the financial freedom he now enjoys. He is a man of God whom I consider my friend, a man who loves God and walks in His ways.

I want you to know that same freedom and liberty regarding your personal finances. It is my prayer that the truths contained in this book will help you leave your "Egypt" of debt and bondage behind and walk into your "Canaan", a place overflowing with the blessings of God.

Benny Hinn
August, 1996

[1]U.S. NEWS & WORLD REPORT, DECEMBER 11, 1995. U.S. NEWS/Bozell poll of 1,009 adults conducted by KRC Research Nov. 3-7, 1995, with consulting by U.S. NEWS pollsters Celinda Lake of Lake Research and Ed Goeas of the Tarrance Group.

Introduction

These few words of introduction, whether they be poetic or crude, will be from my heart. Unedited, unscreened by the stenographer or proofreaders. There is a burning desire on the inside of me to alleviate all the pain, hurt, and disappointment I can in the lives of everyone I can reach. I was raised in poverty and suffered under it in the alleys of a metropolitan jungle for many years. I was touched by what it did to me not only physically, but psychologically and emotionally through severe feelings of inferiority, timidity, and no self-worth. It left me a helpless, crippled orphan at the gate of a world, which for the most part cared very little, but the Good News came, Jesus with His lovely words, ". . . I am come that they might have life, and that they might have it more abundantly" (St. John 10:10). Please do not misunderstand me and what I am about to say as ego or pride. I was a drowning and God got me out of a garbage can and through these little chapters of my testimony. Reader, follow it like a road map. It has brought me self-worth and self-esteem.

I leave you to dive into this book with this one thought and scripture. I wanted out of poverty real bad. It has a special stench of its own. Use this book like a road map. It took me out. Do every word faithfully . . . it is the word of freedom. "I perceive God is not a respecter of persons." Hebrews 6:12 says, "That ye be not slothful, but followers of them who through faith and patience inherit the promises."

Psalm 112: 1-3

Praise ye the Lord. Blessed is the man that feareth the Lord, that delighteth greatly is his commandments.

His seed shall be mighty upon earth: the generation of the upright shall be blessed.

Wealth and riches shall be in his house: and his righteousness endureth for ever.

TABLE OF CONTENTS

Chapter 1

GOD WANTS YOU OUT OF DEBT

America today faces grave economic problems This year the Federal Government will spend 195 billion dollars more than it takes into its treasury. The interest alone on the debt will cost Americans 52 million dollars a day. The 1983 Federal Debt amounted to more than $6,318 per man, woman, and child in America. Since that time the Senate has raised the Federal Debt ceiling.

Statisticians tell us that currently 4% of the nation pays roughly a third of all Federal income tax. Thirty-five percent of the American people are on some form of welfare. What started out to be an aid to people temporarily out of work or unable to work has become a way of life. Welfare now makes up 48.4% of annual Federal expenditures.

Since January, 1985, seventeen commercial banks across America have closed their doors. Nine hundred more are on the FDIC problem list, and the mounting loan losses on farm, real estate and energy loans have caused experts to project that as many as 1,100 banks could be affected. Less than 65% of deposits have been recovered from the banks which have

Since January, 1985, through the calendar year of 1994, over 1,000 commercial banks and savings & loans establishments have been closed or financially assisted, with almost another 300 showing up on the problem bank list of the supervisory authorities. Recent demographics have shown that less than 65% of deposits have been recovered from the banks and S&L's which have already closed.

Americans have not received the message that there is a problem. Like the Federal Government, the private sector also continues to spend more money than they earn. They continue to spend at a rate that is more than double the rate of increase in their personal incomes. Consumer debt accounts for an average of 30% of our annual personal disposable income.

Thus, Americans are saving very little money. Inflation is robbing from the market value of what money is saved. Currently, the value of the dollar is reduced to 0.675 cents. The cost of living has been climbing at a staggering pace. In 1980, 75% of America was priced out of the new housing market. This particular trend has shown improvement, however, not without cost. The Gross Federal Debt absorbs these improvements by even further added debt.

The Federal Government continues to try various solutions to these problems. But, PRAISE GOD, we as Christians do not need to look to the Federal Government for solutions to our financial problems! We can look to the Word of God, the Bible, for our answers.

The grim economic facts listed above are not included in this book to bring fear to you, but rather to point out the problem. You see, for every problem that faces us in life there is a solution in the Word of God.

These statistics may be more than ink on paper to you. You may be one of the millions of Americans so deeply in debt that you cannot see a way out. But, PRAISE GOD, there is a way out of debt through the Word of God.

Romans 12:2 says, "And be not conformed to this world: but be ye transformed by the renewing of your mind, that ye may prove what is that good and acceptable and perfect will of God." The Greek word translated world in this verse is AION. According to *Vine's Expository Dictionary of New Testament Words*, this word means an age or period of time marked by spiritual or moral characteristics. We could say it this way: world means the system of this age in which we live.

Romans 12:2 tells us not to conform to, adapt to, or be a part of this world's system. Why is that? II Corinthians 4:4 tells us that Satan is the god of this world (same Greek word for world is used here). The system of this world is exactly opposite God's system because it is controlled by His archenemy. We who are born again are no longer part of that system. Ephesians 2:2 says that we once walked according to the course of this world, according to the prince of the power of the air, the spirit that now worketh in the children of disobedience. Colossians 1:13 says that we have been translated out of the kingdom of darkness into the kingdom of God's dear Son. Jesus said in John 17:14-16 that we are in the world, but not part of the world. We now belong to the kingdom of God. His kingdom has a system. Those principles are found in the Word of God.

Even though the economic picture coming out of

Washington is very dismal, we as Christians need not be disturbed. We are no longer part of that system. Washington is not our source of supply. God, El Shaddai, the One Who is more than enough, is our source. So look to the hills from whence cometh your help. Get your economic statistics and long-range forecasts from the Bible. God's Word is full of wisdom on how to get out of debt, stay out of debt, and apply financial principles which will bring success.

God's Will Concerning Getting Out of Debt

In order to get out of debt, you must know God's will on the subject. Therefore, let us first of all establish that IT IS GOD'S WILL FOR YOU TO BE OUT OF DEBT.

Owe No Man Anything

Romans 13:8 in the Amplified Translation says, "Keep out of debt and owe no man anything, except to love one another; for he who loves his neighbor—who practices loving others— has fulfilled the Law (relating to one's fellowmen), meeting all its requirements." When we read this verse in context, we see that Paul is talking about finances when he says keep out of debt. Romans 13:6, 7 reads: "For this same reason you pay taxes, for (the civil authorities) are official servants under God, devoting themselves to attending to this very service. Render to all men their dues. (Pay) taxes to whom taxes are due, revenue to whom revenue is due, respect to whom respect is due, and honor to whom honor is due." Paul is talking about paying taxes, rendering dues and paying money to whom it is due. Then, in that same context, in verse 8, he says keep out of debt—that means financial debt.

Deuteronomy 28 gives us some more insight into God's will concerning indebtedness. Let's read verses 11 and 12. "And the

Lord shall make thee plenteous in goods, in the fruit of thy body, and in the fruit of thy cattle, and in the fruit of thy ground, in the land which the Lord sware unto thy fathers to give thee. The Lord shall open unto thee his good treasure, the heaven to give the rain unto thy land in his season, and to bless all the work of thine hand: and thou shalt lend unto many nations, and thou shalt not borrow." Verse 12 says God wants to open up His treasure for you! Think about it. If you had a treasure at your disposal, you wouldn't need to borrow would you? We don't need Household Finance! Why? Because all the treasures of heaven are ours!   And, there is a way to tap into that treasure! Verse 12 goes on to say that we shall lend to many nations and not what?   BORROW!!!   God's will is that we have so much treasure, we not only take care of our own needs, but help others too!

Let's go to Psalm 112 and look at some more scriptures which further establish God's will concerning us NOT being in debt. Verse 1 says: "Praise ye the Lord. Blessed is the man that feareth the Lord, that delighteth greatly in his commandments." This Psalm is written to those who fear God and delight in His Word. The rest of the Psalm tells us things which are true about such a person. Verses 2-5 say, "His seed shall be mighty upon earth: the generation of the upright shall be blessed. Wealth and riches shall be in his house: and his righteousness endureth for ever. Unto the upright there ariseth light in the darkness: He is gracious, and full of compassion, and right-eous. A good man sheweth favor, and lendeth: he will guide his affairs with discretion." Well, folks, if you're lending, then evi-dently you don't need to be borrowing. Why can you lend? Because God's will is that wealth and riches be in the house of those who fear Him and delight in His Word!

Why God Wants You Out of Debt

It may help you to see more clearly that it is God's will for you to be out of debt, if you understand exactly why He wants you out of debt. Let's consider that idea for a moment.

One reason God wants you out of debt is to get financial pressure off you. Let's turn to Philippians 4:4 "Rejoice in the Lord alway: and again I say, "Rejoice." I'm sure you know how hard it is to rejoice when you are under horrible financial pressure. Marriage counselors tell us that sixty to seventy percent of all problems in marriages are financial problems or financial pressure.

One reason God wants you out of debt is so you are not pressed down by the weight of financial pressures.

Philippians 4:5,6 goes on to say, "Let your moderation be known unto all men. The Lord is at hand. Be careful for nothing; but in every thing by prayer and supplication with thanksgiving let your requests be made known unto God." Be careful for nothing means don't be worried about anything!! The Greek word translated care in English is MERIMNA. It means to be anxious about or to be distracted by an engrossing concern. Financial pressure can make it very difficult to obey Philippians 4:6. God does not want you to have the pressure of finances on you. He wants you out of debt so that you can be carefree.

The Danger of Worldly Cares

Another reason God wants you out of debt is because financial pressure can choke the Word of God in your heart. In the fourth chapter of Mark, Jesus compared the Word of God to a seed which is planted in the ground of your heart. But, in verse 19 of that chapter, Jesus says there are things which can choke the Word and stunt its growth in your heart. The cares of this world will choke the Word! Financial pressure due to indebtedness is a care of this world. Folks, the less pressure you have on yourself, the easier it is for you to believe God and take Him at His Word. The easier it is for you to exercise faith. The easier it is for the seed of the Word of God to take root in your heart and grow.

Let me give you an example from my own life. In my early ministry the Lord spoke to me and told me to start doing meetings across the country and rent my own hotels, motels and auditoriums. At that time, I was head over heels in debt and just didn't see how in the world I was going to be able to do it. The budget for a three-day meeting might be $1,800. It was all I could do to fight the fight of faith. The devil would wake me up at three and four o'clock in the morning with the fear that I wouldn't make it. The care of that thing, the worry of it, the pressure of it, was so hard to deal with.

But the more I got out of debt, the easier it was to believe for money to meet my needs. As I got the financial pressure off myself by gradually getting out of debt, more money than ever came in. Why? Because I did not have the care of financial pressure choking the Word in my heart! The Word produced faith in my heart, and I was able to receive the financial blessings God wanted me to have.

The Principle of Sowing and Reaping

One of the best reasons for being out of debt is that you'll be able to give more into the Kingdom to preach the Gospel! You see, God set up a spiritual principle called sowing and reaping. The Bible says that to get, you must first give. God wanted sons and daughters. To get those sons and daughters, God gave or seeded a Son—The Lord Jesus Christ! Proverbs 11:24-26 says, "There is that scattereth, and yet increaseth; and there is that withholdeth more than is meet, but it tendeth to poverty. The liberal soul shall be made fat: and he that watereth shall be watered also himself. He that withholdeth corn, the people shall curse him: but blessing shall be upon the head of him that selleth it." The more you give, the more God is able to bless you because you are cooperating with spiritual law. And the more you are out of debt, the more you'll have to give! And the more seed you plant the larger your harvest will be!

Debt Slaves

Proverbs 22:7 says the borrower is the servant to the lender. I'm sure you realize that we don't need to be in service to anyone but Almighty God! Remember Abraham? He made it clear in Genesis 14:17-24 that he didn't want anybody to be able to say that anyone other than God made him rich. There ought to come a time in our lives when we shake ourselves and arise and look to God as our total source and supplier—not to the government, not to the economy, not to our jobs, but to God! We need to adopt this attitude: "I'm going to make it no matter what the economy does because God supplies all my needs according to His riches—not according to this world's economy, but according to heaven's economy." The number one way to get to that point is to get out of debt.

Romans 12:2 says, "And be not conformed to this world: but be ye transformed by the renewing of your mind, that ye may prove what is that good, and acceptable, and perfect, will of God." God has three wills: His good will, His acceptable will, and His perfect will. God spoke to me and said, "Son, you have no idea how I'm able to pour out My blessings upon you when you get into My perfect will for your life. When you're out of My perfect will, it's not that I don't want to bless you, I can't bless you because the channels are blocked." The moment you get into the perfect will of God, He can double and triple your finances. And, part of being in God's perfect will is getting out of debt and staying out of debt.

Chapter 2

THE LAND OF LACK, THE LAND OF EVEN, AND THE LAND OF PROSPERITY

Several years ago when I realized that God wanted me to get out of debt, I went on a fast. Isaiah 58 lists the rewards of the faster. Two of the rewards mentioned are that your light will spring forth speedily and that you'll be led of the Lord continually. I went into the fast looking for direction from God on how to get out of debt. At that time, I owed about $70,000.

I remember I had just come out of the fast and was in my office praying, when God gave me one of the most marvelous revelations I've ever received. The Word of the Lord came unto me saying, "There are three lands: the Land of Lack, the Land of Even, and the Land of Prosperity. Son, you've seen for a long time that prosperity is My will for you. You've seen that wealth and riches shall be in your house, that you ought to drive what you want to drive and live where you want to live. But son, you're in the Land of Lack and what you've tried to do is live in the Land of Prosperity while you're in the Land of Lack. You've tried to get from Lack to Prosperity without going through the Land of Even."

I realized that was true. I'd buy a car, an expensive one, and buy it on credit. It would be fine for a while, but then I'd have a few low weeks and I'd end up having to sell the car. Up and down, up and down I went. When the Lord spoke to me, I saw for the first time that I was going to have to go through the Land of Even to get to the Land of Prosperity.

God continued instructing me. He said, "Son, keep prosperity before you. But you're going to have to make this your goal right now: that you are going to get to the Land of Even. The Land of Even is where you owe no man anything but to love him. The Land of Even is a wonderful place because you are even with the world and owe nothing and all the pressure is off. After you reach that point it's easy to step into the Land of Prosperity. Once you get to the Land of Even, it's easy to be a dollar ahead in everything instead of a dollar behind."

No doubt, a lot of you are like I was—trying to get to the Land of Prosperity from the Land of Lack without first going through the Land of Even. Make the decision to get to the Land of Even where you owe no man anything!

Before we move on to practical "how to's of getting out of debt," I'd like to spend a little time on a very important point. Most people would agree that it is good to live in the Land of Even, that place where you owe no man anything but to love him. However, many people have a problem with the idea that God wants His children to prosper financially. Many Christians have religious ideas about money which are unscriptural. Not only is it God's will for you to be out of debt, it is His will for you to prosper! I want to show you from the Word of God that it is His will to bless you financially. You will never get to the Land of Prosperity unless you first know that you have the right to be there.

I've heard well-meaning Christians make this statement: "God doesn't want us to have money because the Bible says that money is the root of all evil." That is a misquote of I Timothy 6:10. This verse actually says that the LOVE OF MONEY is the root of all evil. Money in and of itself is not evil. It is neutral. Our attitude toward money determines whether it is good or bad for us. We are not to love money, we are to love God. We are not to trust in our money, we are to trust in God. God is not against you having money. He is against money having you. Did you know that you can have the love of money and not have a dime? I've met people like that.

When discussing the subject of financial prosperity, many people refer to the story of the rich young ruler found in the Gospels. He came to Jesus asking what he must do to inherit eternal life. After a little conversation, Jesus told the man to sell all his possessions. People use this incident as proof that God does not want us to have material blessings in this life. They quote Mark 10:23 where Jesus says, "How hardly shall they that have riches enter into the kingdom of God," and point out the fact that riches can keep you out of heaven.

But, if we read the entire passage, we find that that is not at all what Jesus is saying. In Mark 10:24 Jesus continues with this statement: "Children, how hard it is for them that TRUST IN RICHES to enter into the kingdom of God." Jesus is telling us that the problem is not with the riches themselves, but with riches. Jesus obviously discerned that this young man was trusting in and relying upon his riches rather than God. His riches were a stumbling block to that particular man because he trusted in them. Once again we see the same theme which we found in I Timothy 6:10. Money is not evil. Trusting in money and its power rather than in the power of God is evil.

In Mark 4:19 Jesus said that one of the things which can stop the Word of God from growing in our hearts is the deceitfulness of riches. Jesus did not say that riches can hurt our spiritual growth, but rather their deceitfulness The New English Translation of that verse calls it the "false glamour of riches." Riches can deceive you; they can mislead you—if you begin to trust in and rely upon them rather than upon God.

There are pitfalls in riches. But, thank God, we have the Bible and the Holy Spirit to teach us how to avoid those pitfalls. To be forewarned is to be forearmed. Before you enter the Land of Prosperity, make the decision that you will never allow money to get in the way of your relationship with God.

Let's take time to look at some scriptures which clearly state that financial prosperity is God's will for His children. III John 2 says, "Beloved, I wish above all things that thou mayest PROSPER and be in health, even as thy soul PROSPERETH." According to this verse, as our soul or inner man grows and develops, there ought to be a corresponding growth and success in our physical and material lives. Psalm 35:27 says the Lord "hath pleasure in the PROSPERITY of his servant."

Joshua 1:8 says, "This book of the law (the Word of God) shall not depart out of thy mouth; but thou shalt meditate therein day and night, that thou mayest observe to do according to all that is written therein: for then thou shalt make thy way PROSPEROUS, and then thou shalt have good success." This verse gives us instructions on how to be prosperous and successful—by meditating on the Word of God day and night and doing what it says. If prosperity is against God's will, why did He give us instructions on how to become prosperous?

Some people might say, "How do you know the word prosperous refers to money?" How do you know it doesn't? Most of us have been so religiously brainwashed that whenever we see anything in the Bible that suggests financial prosperity, we automatically begin to reason why such and such a scripture can't possibly be referring to money! Think about it for a minute. If I describe someone to you as being a prosperous man, you know exactly what I mean. I'm telling you that the man is well-off financially!! We have no right to alter the meaning of words selected by the Holy Ghost in order to fit our religious tradition—especially when other verses in the Bible make it clear that financial prosperity is a blessing from God.

Psalm 112 is a description of a man who fears God and delights in His commandments. Verse 3 makes this statement about such a man: "Wealth and riches shall be in his house." God's will for the godly man is that wealth and riches— MONEY—be in his house.

Psalm 24:1 says, "The earth is the Lord's, and the fullness thereof." That means all the oil reserves, the gold deposits, the veins of silver, the diamonds, emeralds and rubies hidden in the earth belong to God. Why would our heavenly Father be unwilling to share His wealth with His children? God has already demonstrated to us that He is a giver. John 3:16 tells us that God loved us so much that He gave us Jesus. Romans 8:32 says, "He that spared not his own Son, but delivered him up for us all, how shall He not with him also FREELY GIVE US ALL THINGS?" The answer to that question is He *will* give to us freely.

What earthly father is there who would withhold from his children something they need or want if it is in his power to supply it? Jesus Himself used that comparison in Matthew 7:11. He said, "If ye then, being evil (or natural), know how to give good gifts unto your children, how much more shall your Father which is in heaven give good things to them that ask him?"

God, Who owns the cattle upon a thousand hills according to Psalm 50:10, did not put all this fabulous wealth into the earth for the devil and his crowd. The gold and the silver were not placed on this earth to provide money for movie stars to have cocaine parties on yachts. It was placed here for God's children so that we can PREACH THE GOSPEL, (it takes money to preach the Gospel) and so that we may be able to have FULL PROVISION. Jesus said in John 10:10, "I am come that they might have life, and that they might have it more abundantly." God's will for you is ABUNDANT LIFE!!

Proverbs 13:22 says, "A good man leaveth an inheritance to his children's children: and the wealth of the sinner is laid up for the just." The first part of the verse points out that a good man leaves an inheritance to his children's children. You have to have a fair amount of money to leave an inheritance to begin with, but you must have a substantial amount to leave some to your grandchildren as well as your own children.

The second part of Proverbs 13:22 further establishes the point we made above. The massive amounts of wealth on this earth were not meant for the sinner. They were meant for the children of God. When the children of Israel left Egypt (a type of the world) they took with them gold, silver, jewels and fine clothing according to Exodus 12:35,36. The wealth of the sinners went to the chosen of God. It's time we started claiming our blessings too!

There are a lot more scriptures revealing God's will concerning prosperity than we can possibly cover in just one chapter. But before we move on, let's consider one more point—our covenant relationship with God.

In Genesis 17 God appeared to Abraham and entered into a covenant agreement with him. God promised Abraham that if he walked sprightly before Him in obedience and sincerity of heart, God would make him the father of many nations and through him all nations would be blessed. The physical sign of the covenant agreement was the circumcision of every male child.

As we study the rest of Abraham's life, we find that one of the blessings of his covenant relationship with God was financial prosperity. Abraham died a very wealthy man. A study of the life of his son Isaac and his grandson Jacob reveals the same thing. They were extremely wealthy men because of their covenant relationship with God. You can read their stories for yourself in the rest of the Book of Genesis!

When the Law was given to the children of Israel some 700 years after Abraham established the original covenant, financial blessing continued to be a benefit of their relationship with God. Deuteronomy 28 lists the blessings promised to those who keep the law as well as the curses which result from disobedience. As we read that chapter, we find financial blessings referred to numerous times.

Deuteronomy 8:18 says, "But thou shalt remember the Lord thy God: for it is he that giveth thee power to get wealth, that he may establish his covenant which he sware unto thy fathers, as it is this day." God gives those with whom He has a covenant relationship the power to get wealth! Why? So that He can establish His covenant! What does that mean? It means that He gives people power to get wealth so that He can hold up His end of the bargain! A covenant is a two-party agreement under which both parties commit to do certain things. Under the old covenant one of the things God committed to do was meet all of the physical needs of the children of Israel. To fulfill His part of the agreement, He gave them the power to get money!

Christians today also have a covenant agreement with God. It is called the New Covenant. It was established through the death, burial and resurrection of Jesus Christ. We enter the covenant when we are born again. Hebrews 8:6 tells us that this new covenant which we have with God is "a better covenant, which was established on better promises."

If financial prosperity was part of the first or old covenant between God and man—and it clearly was— and this new covenant is a better agreement according to Hebrews 8:6, then financial prosperity must be a part of this covenant also. It's very clear that it would not be a *better* covenant if it provided us with less than the old covenant provided for the children of Israel. Financial prosperity *is* part of the new covenant and you have a right to it just as much as any other covenant blessing.

Even though we've only scratched the surface on the subject, I believe that you can see from the scriptures discussed that financial prosperity is part of God's will for His children. It is God's will that you enter into the Land of Prosperity and dwell there. Now that you know you have a right to enter the Land of Prosperity, let's find out how to get from the Land of Lack to the Land of Even and ultimately to the Land of Prosperity!

Chapter 3

THERE IS A WAY OUT

There is a way to get out of debt. There are a number of things you can do both in the spiritual and in the natural to get out of debt. I'd like to share with you some of the things my family did to get out from under almost $70,000 worth of debt.

The first thing you must do is to realize that the Holy Spirit, the great Teacher and Guide of the Church, will teach you how to get out of debt and lead you into the Land of Even. Depend on Him to lead you and guide you and direct you. He knows the quickest way for you to get out of debt. He knows where you are wasting money. Ask Him to show you where you need to make changes and how to make them. He'll show you things around the house for which you have no use that you can sell to make money.

The Holy Spirit will help you make the right investments. He'll help you guide your affairs with discretion. He'll show you how to get some extra money together to make extra principal payments on your home. Even that small step can make a tremendous difference in your financial condition. There is a way out of debt, and the Holly Spirit will give you tips on how to do it as you look to Him for help. With that in mind, let me give you five practical rules which God has shown me over the years on how to get out of debt.

Rule #1: Set A Goal

Rule number one in getting out of debt is setting a goal or establishing a vision for yourself. Several years ago when the Lord told me that it was His will for me to get out of debt and head for the Land of Even, because He wanted me to get to the Land of Prosperity, I had no hope. I had no hope whatsoever of getting out of debt. I could not even see a way out. Everybody I knew was in debt. My whole family was in debt. We never bought anything in my family without borrowing the money for it. I never knew any other way. I did not know there was any other way to live. But, Praise God, there is another way to live!

One of the hardest, yet most important, things I ever did was to get my mind, my head and my heart renewed with the Word of God until I really believed that there was another way to live. I never even imagined that I could own a car and actually have the title in my hands! God had to renew my mind and get the vision on the inside of me that it was actually possible to own something, to pay cash, to quit borrowing. You will never get out of debt until you come to the point where you really believe that it can happen to you too.

Proverbs 29:18 says, "Where there is no vision, the people perish." You need a vision to get out of debt. You are going to have to get a vision of yourself paying cash. See yourself or imagine yourself out of debt. God said to me, "Son, I want you to get a hope for this; I want you to get a vision of it. I want you to set this as your goal—to get out of debt." So, my wife and I and the kids got together and we set our goal. Our goal for many years had been to walk in divine health. And I remember when we hit that. But this time I said, "Our goal is to get completely out of debt and to move toward divine prosperity. And we are headed, our faces set like a flint, toward that goal in the Name of Jesus Christ. We believe it is possible to do it, Praise God!" You are going to have to do the same thing if you want to get out of debt. Set a goal. Get the vision of yourself out of debt.

It is God's will that you be out of debt -- that you control your finances instead of your finances controlling you.

Rule #2: Make A List

One key step in getting out of debt is to make a list of all the debts you owe. Then pay off the list one debt at a time. Don't try to attack the whole debt at one time. PAY IT OFF LINE BY LINE.

The next thing God told me to do to get out of debt was to make a list of everything I owed. You need to do the same thing. That list should include credit cards, revolving charge accounts, debts to friends, debts to family—in other words—EVERYTHING. We made our list and wrote the amount owed next to each one. It was quite a list—twenty or twenty-five debts. Then, after we made the list, we took one bill as our goal and headed toward that goal. Once we got that bill paid off, we moved down the list and set a new goal. Everything that came in above what it took for the budget of the ministry, we put toward paying off that bill until we were able to cross it off the list.

Now it may seem as though you are so far in debt and have so many bills, that there is no way out. But you have to walk in patience, and once you get God involved in it, it really doesn't take that long. It may take some of you a year or even two years or more to get out of debt. Time is going to pass anyway so you might as well put it to good use. We just patiently worked our way down the list, all the time believing God to help us pay off our debts. Even in our giving we gave toward the goal of being completely out of debt. Whether we gave to a ministry or to people, we would say, "Father, this is toward our goal of heading toward the Land of Even. We are investing in other ministries and planting seeds toward being out of debt."

Sometimes I'd get that list out and just look at it. It gave me great joy to look at what we had already scratched out and to see where we were headed. I'll tell you what, that list was a point of contact for our faith. Sometimes, we'd walk around in shopping centers and when we'd start to buy something we didn't have the money for, I'd say, "No, it would just make the list longer Praise God, I can be happier looking at that list than I can buying these shoes I don't have the money for right now." It would help build my resistance and the next time I would be tempted to buy something I could not afford, it would be easier for me to resist.

Don't try to look at the overall debt; it would be staggering and would discourage you. Pick one debt at a time and set it as your goal. Work toward erasing your debts a line at a time on your list. When the devil comes against you saying that there is no hope, you tell him that there is hope because the God of hope is helping you pay off your debts.

Rule #3: Add No New Debts

Add no new debts while you pay off the debts on your list. To get to the Land of Even, you are going to have to spend evenly—that means not spending more than you have. *Make the decision* to add no new debts. Now that does not mean that you can't have anything while you pay off your debts. If you want something, use it as a faith project. Believe God for the thing or for the cash to buy it. If you want a refrigerator, a coffee table, a bicycle or whatsoever, use your faith to pull it in. Don't go further into debt. It is possible to do that, isn't it? Of course it is! The Bible says the just shall *live* by faith!

God will do some marvelous things for your financially when you make the decision to get out of debt by the power of God. I heard Brother Kenneth Copeland make this statement: "If I can't get it with my faith, I don't even want it in my house!" It took awhile, but that idea has become a way of life for my family and me. You can walk in my house and see the results of faith in every room and I didn't borrow a dime to get it. I used my faith for it. Everything in our house is a testimony. I can walk around and look at things God has given us and I appreciate everything He has done.

Several years ago my wife and I needed a bedroom suite. We made the decision to believe God for it and not borrow any money. I had no sooner spoken the words that God would provide it for us, when the phone rang. It was a man from Chicago who told me the Lord told him to buy my wife and me a bedroom suite! He was writing out the check as he spoke on the phone. Two days later, the check arrived in the mail! Isn't that wonderful? I could tell you testimony after testimony where that has happened over and over again. God is no respecter of persons and what He has done for us He will do for you—but you must use your faith.

My family and I have made the decision, by the power of the Holy Spirit, to stay out of debt! And I believe that I will not lack or do without as a result of that decision. I'm headed towards God's best. If you are in debt now, don't be under any condemnation about it, but make your decision to get out of debt.

Rule #4: Set A Time For Your Goal

Set a time for your goal. Pick a particular bill—whatever number you have reached on your list—and say, "I believe I am going to have this bill paid off in thirty days." Perhaps if it a very large bill, you may have to set a sixty day limit. But set a time on that bill. It will help you keep the pressure on yourself to continue moving toward your goal.

Rule #5: Singleness of Purpose

If you ever expect to get out of debt and to get over into the Land of Prosperity, you are going to have to have a single purpose. You'll have to be single-minded. That means you must decide to head toward getting out of debt and never turn the other way. James 1:2 says, "My brethren, count it all joy when ye fall into divers temptations; knowing this, that the trying of your faith worketh patience." When you make the decision to get out of debt, the devil will tempt you to back down from that stand. God showed me something very interesting about temptations. Just like some people are tempted to eat when they aren't hungry, others are tempted to buy when they don't really need anything. Don't yield to those temptations. Use the Name of Jesus on them. Don't allow them to move you away from your purpose—getting out of debt.

Don't yield to the temptation to buy. Go back to your debt list and say, "Praise God; that's where I'm headed—out of debt." Remind yourself that they always have cars for sale; they always have houses for sale. You can buy those things once you reach your goal. Boldly declare: "I'm headed for the Land of Prosperity which God says is available. I'm going to have all these things, but I'm going to have them by the power of the Holy Spirit."

James 1:3,4 goes on to say, "Knowing this, that the trying of your faith worketh patience. But let patience have her perfect work, that ye may be perfect and entire, wanting nothing." Do you know that if you will be patient, you will want for nothing? That is what the Bible says right here, doesn't it? If you'll exercise patience as you work toward getting out of debt, YOU WILL MAKE IT!

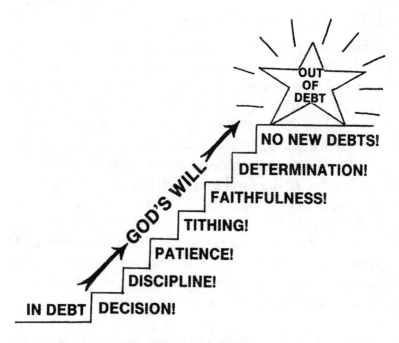

You won't get out of debt overnight. But if you take it step-by-step and apply the principles of God's Word, you will reach your goal.

James 1:5-8 continues, "If any of you lack wisdom, let him ask of God, that giveth to all men liberally, and upbraideth not; and it shall be given him. But let him ask in faith, nothing wavering. For he that wavereth is like a wave of the sea driven with the wind and tossed. For let not that man think that he shall receive anything of the Lord. A double minded man is unstable in all his ways." It takes a quality decision to get out of debt. Satan will never allow you to get out of debt unless you commit to singleness of purpose, until you make the decision to be unwavering. You must say, "I'll not be moved! I'll not be led to the left nor to the right, for I am headed out of debt." Set that as your goal in life. Somewhere down the road, you are going to have to make the decision that it is possible to get out of debt. Then you must say and do the things the Bible says to get there.

Chapter

TITHING TODAY

In order get out of debt, you are going to have to learn to cooperate with God's basic principles. As we mentioned earlier, God has set up certain spiritual laws concerning giving and receiving. When you give, you open up the channels in your life through which God can bless you. Since tithing is so important to our financial well-being, we need to look at it in depth. Let's begin by looking at the biblical history of tithing.

Tithing Was Instituted Before the Law

Let's look at Genesis 14:17-20. "And the king of Sodom went out to meet him after his return from the slaughter of Chedorlaomer, and of the kings that were with him, at the valley of Shaveh, which is the king's dale. And Melchizedek king of Salem brought forth bread and wine: and he was the priest of the most high God. And he blessed him, and said, Blessed be Abram of the most high God, possessor of heaven and earth: and blessed be the most high God, which hath delivered thine enemies into thy hand. And he gave him tithes of all."

The events described in this passage took place seven hundred years before God gave the Law to Moses. Upon returning from a battle in which he defeated Chedorlaomer, king of Elam, Abram was met by Melchizedek, the priest of God. Verse 20 tells us that Abram gave a tenth or a tithe of all the spoils of war to the priest of the most high God. There was no requirement or law which said that Abram had to give to God. Abram simply chose to give God a tithe or a tenth of all the spoils of war by giving it to the priest of God. Abram didn't have to do it, but he made a quality decision to do so.

Verses 21-24 go on to say, "And the king of Sodom said unto Abram, Give me the persons, and take the goods to thyself. And Abram said to the king of Sodom, I have lift up mine hand unto the Lord, the most high God, the possessor of heaven and earth. That I will not take from a thread even to a shoelatchet, and that I will not take any thing that is thine, lest thou shouldest say, I have made Abram rich: Save only that which the young men have eaten, and the portion of the men which went with me."

These verses tell us of another decision Abram made. The king of Sodom told Abram he could keep all the material goods taken in the battle. Abram refused the offer. Abram said that he had made an oath to God that he would accept nothing from the king of Sodom because he did not want the king to have the opportunity to say, "I made Abram rich." Abram knew, and he wanted everyone else to know, that God was his source of supply. If anyone made Abram rich, it would be God.

In this first Biblical example of tithing we see a man who freely chose to give God a tenth of all because he recognized God as his only source of material supply! What kind of results did this attitude produce in Abram's life? Genesis 17 tells us that God changed this man's name to Abraham and entered into a covenant with him, promising Abraham that he would become the father of many nations. That covenant became what we call the Old Covenant. As we study the rest of Abraham's life we find that he was exceedingly blessed by God, materially as well as spiritually. God promised Abraham the land of Canaan and made him extremely wealthy. Also, through His covenant with Abraham, God established the lineage or family out of which Jesus would be born.

Jacob and Tithing

So Abraham made the decision to tithe and one result was that God made a covenant with Abraham and blessed him mightily. From Abraham came a child by the name of Isaac and from Isaac came Jacob. Let's read about Abraham's grandchild Jacob in Genesis 28:18-22. Jacob lived some 500 years before the Law of Moses was given. "And Jacob rose up early in the morning, and took the stone that he had put for his pillows, and set it up for a pillar, and poured oil upon the top of it. And he called the name of that place Bethel: but the name of that city was called Luz at the first. And Jacob vowed a vow, saying, If God will be with me, and will keep me in this way that I go, and will give me bread to eat, and raiment to put on, So that I come again to my father's house in peace; then shall the Lord be my God: and this stone, which I have set for a pillar, shall be God's house: and of all that thou shalt give me I will surely give the tenth unto thee."

Jacob also made a vow to give God a tenth of all he had. He voluntarily chose to give a tithe unto God! If you study the life of Jacob in the Bible you will see that he too was phenomenally blessed by God. He learned the secret his grandfather Abraham knew about recognizing God as his source. He, no doubt, made a vow based on what he had seen working for his daddy, Isaac, the richest man around who also applied the same principles as Abraham. Jacob chose to give God a tenth of all he had.

Tithing Under the Law

The practice of tithing was not done away with when God gave the Law to Moses. As we study the Old Testament, we find that tithing became a part of the Law. There are too many scriptures for us to consider now, but let us look at a few. Leviticus 27:30 says, "And all the tithe of the land, whether of the seed of the land, or of the fruit of the tree, is the Lord's: it is holy unto the Lord." Deuteronomy 14:22 says, "Thou shalt truly tithe all the increase of thy seed, that the field bringeth forth year by year."

The children of Israel tithed under the reign of Hezekiah. II Chronicles 31:5 says, "And as soon as the commandment came abroad, the children of Israel brought in abundance the first-fruits of corn, wine, and oil, and honey, and of all the increase of the field; and the tithe of all things brought they in abundantly."

In the book of Nehemiah we find another reference to tithing. Chapter 10 verse 37 says, "And that we should bring the firstfruits of our dough, and our offerings, and the fruit of all manner of trees, of wine and of oil, unto the priests, to the chambers of the house of our God; and the tithes of our ground unto the Levites, that the same Levites might have the tithes in all the cities of our tillage." Numerous other examples of tithing are found under the Old Covenant.

Tithing in the New Testament

Some people say that tithing was an Old Covenant practice,

and that there is no reason for New Testament believers to continue tithing. There are two errors in that line of reasoning. We have just seen from our examination of Abraham and Jacob that tithing existed *before* the law was instituted. That means tithing was not limited just to people living under the law. We also learned from our study that both men began to tithe, not as a result of a direct command from God, but as the result of a quality decision each of them made to recognize God as their source of all. What does that mean? It means that tithing can and does exist apart from the law and that tithing isn't necessarily a response to a command from God. All of this means that tithing *can* be a New Testament practice.

The second error in the idea that tithing is not a New Covenant practice is the fact that tithing is found in the New Testament. Let's look at Hebrews Chapter 7. In Chapter 7, the writer of Hebrews is talking about Jesus as our high priest. Hebrews 6:20 says that "Jesus (was) made an high priest for ever after the order of Melchizedec." The priesthood of Christ is compared to the priesthood of Melchizedec, the one to whom Abraham paid his tithes in Genesis 14.

If Christ's priesthood is like Melchizedek's priesthood, then we need to know some facts about Melchizedek's priesthood. First, he was not part of the Levitical priesthood set up under the law (that is, Levi and his descendants). Secondly, Abraham did not give tithes to Melchizedec because it was the law (the law was not yet established) or because God told him to do so. Abraham chose to do it. Thirdly, the priesthood of Melchizedec was greater than that of the Levites. Hebrews 7:4 says, "Now consider how great this man (Melchizedec) was, unto whom even the patriarch Abraham gave the tenth of the spoils." Verses 5 through 9 make the point that the Levites were *descendants* of Abraham. Because the Levites were not yet born when Abraham paid tithes, Levi and his descendants were still in Abraham, inside his loins. So according to verse 9, Levi, because he was still in Abraham, being yet unborn, actually paid tithes to Melchizedec. The lesser priest paid tithes to the greater priest.

How does all of that relate to Christ? One of the main points of the entire letter to the Hebrews is that the priesthood of Christ is greater than the priesthood of the Levites. We just read in Hebrews 6:20 that Christ's priesthood is like unto Melchizedek's. Since Abraham paid tithes to Melchizedec because he was worthy of the honor, and Christ is a priest after the order of Melchizedec, then New Covenant believers ought to pay tithes to our high priest, Jesus Christ, because HE IS CERTAINLY WORTHY OF THE HONOR.

Abraham made a free will choice to tithe to our high priest, Jesus Christ. II Corinthians 9:7 (talking about money) says, "Every man according as he purposeth in his heart, so let him give; not grudgingly, or of necessity: for God loveth a cheerful giver." This verse tells us to purpose or choose to give money. Choosing to give money *is* a New Testament practice. Abraham's tithe was a choice. *Choose* to give tithes to Jesus Christ because He is our high priest just as Melchizedec was Abraham's high priest.

Hebrews 7:8 says, "And here men that die receive tithes; but there he receiveth them, of whom it is witnessed that he liveth." This scripture contrasts paying tithes to those who die—the Levites—to one who lives. Who is the One that liveth and abideth forever? The Lord Jesus Christ! We are to make a quality decision to tithe unto the One who lives forever!

Chapter 5

REWARDS OF THE TITHER

Malachi 3:10 says, "Bring ye all tithes into the storehouse." Tithing is a
Biblical practice. There are great rewards connected with faithful tithing.

There are certain rewards promised to those who tithe. Malachi 3:10 says, "Bring ye all the tithes into the storehouse, that there may be meat in mine house, and prove me now herewith, saith the Lord of hosts, if I will not open you the windows of heaven, and pour you out a blessing, that there shall not be room enough to receive it." God says right here in this verse that if we tithe, He will open up the windows of heaven and pour down on us blessings which are so great, we will not be able to hold them all! He is clearly referring to financial blessings in this verse because the context of the whole passage is financial—he is talking about tithing! Meditate on this scripture. Think about the fact that God wants to pour more blessings on you than you can contain! What a wonderful promise from God!

Notice two key words in this verse: PROVE ME. God is actually saying to the one who tithes, "Prove me or test me in this! Just watch what I'll do when you tithe! I'll open the windows of heaven on you and pour out blessings." GLORY TO GOD!

Malachi 3:11 mentions another reward promised to the tither. "And I will rebuke the devourer for your sakes, and he shall not destroy the fruits of your ground; neither shall your vine cast her fruit before the time in the field, saith the Lord of hosts." God says He will rebuke the devourer for the sake of the person who tithes. The devourer is the devil who comes to kill, steal and destroy. In other places in the Bible, God tells us to use our own authority and rebuke the devil. But to the tither the Lord promises that He will personally rebuke the devourer.

This is such an important promise. Think about it. Even if you were extremely wealthy, your money could be devoured. There are so many areas where the devourer can get your money: home repairs, auto repairs, worn out clothing, etc. But when the devourer is rebuked for your sakes, you can expect your car to last longer; your clothing to last longer! Use your faith in this area. Expect it to happen! There are many examples in the Bible where material things lasted longer by the power of God. Jesus stretched five loaves and two fishes in Mark 6. The widow gave the man of God all of her meal or grain and as a result her meal barrel and oil barrel never did run dry in I Kings 17. God will do things like that for the person who tithes.

A Curse

Just as there are great blessings connected with tithing, there are serious consequences for those who do not tithe. Not paying tithes is a very serious matter. When a person does not pay his tithes, he is withholding from God. Malachi 3:8 actually calls it robbing God! "Will a man rob God? Yet ye have robbed me. But ye say, wherein have we robbed thee? In tithes and offerings." Verse 9 goes on to say, "Ye are cursed with a curse: for ye have robbed me, even this whole nation." The result of not paying tithes is a curse in your life. According to the Bible, the curse is poverty, sickness, and death. By not paying tithes, you open the door of your life to poverty, sickness, and death.

The seventh chapter of the Book of Joshua gives us a vivid example of the consequences of holding back tithes from God. The Israelites marched on the city of Ai and were badly and unexpectedly defeated. Joshua fell on his knees before God in sackcloth and ashes to find out why the defeat took place. God spoke to Joshua and told him the defeat happened because there was sin or disobedience in the Israeli camp.

When Joshua got to the bottom of it at the direction of the Lord, he discovered that one of his men, Achan, had taken 200 shekels of silver and 50 shekels of gold, the spoils of a previous battle, and had hidden them in the ground beneath his tent. Achan took money that should have gone to God. As a result of his sin, Achan was stoned to death and all of his possessions were burned. Robbing from God will stop the blessings of God and open up the door to a curse in your life.

The Tither's Prayer

Once you make the decision to tithe, the way in which you tithe, as well as the attitude of your heart when you tithe, becomes important. We've already looked at II Corinthians 9:7 which tells us that God loves a cheerful giver. But there are other things to remember as well. In Deuteronomy 26:3-16, we find what might be called the tither's prayer. These verses contain six specific instructions for the tither as he brings his tithe to the house of God. Let's briefly consider them.

Step 1: Confess Your Trust in God

Verses 1 and 2 set the stage by telling us that the first fruits or tithes are to be taken to the priest of God. Verse 3 gives us step number one. "And thou shalt go unto the priest that shall be in those days, and say unto him, I profess this day unto the Lord thy God..." When you tithe, don't just drop your money in the bucket without thinking. Make a conscious decision to give it as a profession or confession of faith and trust in God! Don't just go through the motions. Use the offering time as an opportunity to profess your faith in God afresh and anew.

Step 2: Remember the Good Things God Has Done for You

Verses 5-9 give us step two. Verse 5 begins this way: "Thou shalt speak and say before the Lord thy God..." The rest of the passage goes on to list a brief history of the children of Israel from their slavery in Egypt until God brought them into the land of milk and honey. What does all that mean to the tither? It means that as you tithe, remember all the good things God has done for you. You were once a sinner, dead in trespasses and sin, living under the curse of poverty, sickness, and death. But now, because Jesus paid the price you owed and became a curse for you, you've been translated or moved out of the kingdom of darkness and brought into the kingdom of God!

Step 3: Have a Right Attitude

The first part of verse 10 shows us the third step or attitude with which you should bring your tithes to God. "And now, behold, I have brought the firstfruits of the land, which thou, O Lord, hast given me." As you give your tithes to God, recognize the fact that you are only giving back to Him out of what He first gave to you. It all belongs to Him anyway. I Corinthians 4:7 says, "What hast thou that thou didst not receive?" He asks only that you return a tenth of it to Him.

Step 4: Worship

Step four is found in the last part of verse 10. "And thou shalt set it before the Lord thy God, and worship before the Lord thy God." Worship God with your tithes. Tithing is a form of worship. When you worship God you give to Him.

When you tithe to God you are giving to Him out of the time, sweat, and toil it took to earn that money. Offering time is not to be taken lightly. It is a time to worship God.

Step 5: Rejoice!

Verse 11 says, "And thou shalt rejoice in every good thing which the Lord thy God hath given unto thee, and unto thine house." This is step five. Once you've given your tithe, begin to rejoice. Be joyful and thankful! Begin to thank God for what He has already done and for what He is going to do! Be happy about it!

Step 6: Expect a Blessing

The sixth step is just as important as the first five! EXPECT a blessing from God because you have been obedient and given your tithes! That may seem a little presumptuous, but let's see what the Bible says. In verses 13 and 14 the tither states his case, so to speak. He makes mention of the fact that he has been obedient and done what the Lord said concerning tithing. Verse 15 says, "Look down from thy holy habitation, from heaven, and bless thy people Israel..." According to verses 13, 14 and 15, the tither actually has the right to say to God, "I've done my part by paying my tithes; now You, God, do Your part and bless me."

That should be your attitude when you tithe! You may think that sounds too forward with God. But remember Malachi 3. God Himself tells us in that chapter to prove Him or put Him to the test when we tithe and see whether He'll do what He said concerning blessing us. You see, God honors faith! Faith opens the door to God's power in our lives. Faith is agreeing with God. Faith is taking God at His Word. Faith is doing what He says—even in the area of tithing. Faith in the area of tithing means believing what God said in Malachi 3 and EXPECTING HIM TO BLESS YOU. Purpose in your heart to keep His commands and then to expect God to look down on you and bless you in your giving.

Where to Tithe

Where you tithe is just as important as how you tithe. The Bible gives us some guidelines about where to tithe. Malachi 3:10 tells us to bring the tithe into the storehouse. A storehouse is a place where food is found. What does that mean? You are to tithe at the place where you receive your spiritual food, the Word of God.

Deuteronomy 26:2 tells the tither to take his tithe "unto the place which the Lord thy God shall choose to place his name there." The Bible makes many references to places where the Lord chose to put His Name and His Spirit. It also mentions places from which the Spirit of the Lord has departed. God's blessing is not upon every place that calls itself a church. Do not tithe at a dead church. What is a dead church? A church that does not teach the new birth. If such a place is not teaching the new birth, there will be no life there. Giving to such a place is like giving money to the dead. In Deuteronomy 26:14 one of the things the tither points out to God concerning his obedience to the laws of God is that he did not give any of his tithe to the dead. Don't you do it either. Make sure you tithe at a place where God has chosen to put His Name and His Spirit.

We must mention one more point about tithing. WHAT YOU TITHE IS IMPORTANT. WE TEND TO THINK OF TITHES AS MONEY. Money is a part of it. You are to give a tithe of the salary you earn. But if you remember the men we studied in the Bible who tithed, they gave a tenth of *all* that God blessed them with—not just money. You can tithe books, tapes, food, clothing, cars, anything that God gives you.

We made a decision several years ago to give a tithe on everything we received. If someone gave us clothes, for example, we'd figure out the approximate value and then give a money tithe on that. Tithing has worked for us because we are blessed beyond our wildest dreams.

Conclusion

You will never get out of debt unless you make the decision to tithe. Our natural mind tells us that we can't possibly pay tithes when we owe money to others. Or our mind says that we should wait and pay our tithes after we pay off our debts. But, the Bible calls the tithe *firstfruits*. And it is clear from Malachi 3 that a person who does not tithe will be a sitting duck for the devourer. What money you finally scrape together to pay the Sears bill will be eaten up when the car breaks down or when the kids get sick and have to visit the doctor.

Faithful tithing is a vital key to getting out of debt because it opens up the windows of heaven in your life. Through those windows will come the very money you need to get out of debt. When you tithe you give God the opportunity to bless you materially and help you get out of debt.

One of the rewards of faithful tithing is that God will open up the windows of heaven and pour out a blessing which is greater than you can contain.

Chapter

PAYING OFF
YOUR HOME

One vital key to getting out of debt is paying off your home mortgage ahead of schedule. Most people have no idea that they can pay off their home mortgage early. It has been engraved into our thinking that it takes twenty to thirty years to pay for a house. Yet not only is it possible to pay off your mortgage long before that time, it is highly desirable to do so. Let me explain.

Your monthly house payment is made up of two parts: the principal and the interest. The principal is the part of the payment which actually pays for the house. It is the part which reduces the amount you owe on the house. The interest is the part which goes to the banker. It is his profit. It does not reduce the amount of money you owe for your house by one penny. Together, these two components—principal and interest—make up your total monthly payment.

Most people are not aware of how these two parts that make up the monthly payment are divided. People are not aware of how much of their payment is interest and how much is principal. Many people assume that if the interest rate on their loan is 11%, then on each monthly payment, 11% of the money due pays for interest and the rest goes toward the actual amount of the loan. Nothing could be further from the truth. Most people don't realize that for the first half of the term of the loan the greatest part of each monthly payment goes toward interest and not toward paying off the actual amount owed for the house. (The period of time it will take to pay off a loan is called the term of the loan.)

MONTHLY HOUSE PAYMENT

The majority of your monthly house payment goes toward paying interest and not toward paying the principal—the money you actually owe. Early principal payments will solve this problem.

Most people don't realize that the two parts of their payment—principal and interest—are not even equal in amount until halfway through the term of the loan. Before the halfway point in repaying a loan, more money goes to paying the interest than it does to paying the principal. After the halfway point (15 years on a 30 year loan) the greater amount goes toward the principal and the lesser amount goes toward interest. As a result, the majority of the amount of money paid in monthly payments on the first half of a mortgage is interest or profit to the bankers.

Let's look at an actual home mortgage monthly payment schedule known as an amortization schedule. (To amortize means to completely pay off your mortgage.) The amortization schedule shown below is for a mortgage of $88,000 amortized or paid off over 30 years at 11.5% interest with a level monthly payment of $872 (A level payment is a monthly payment which remains the same amount the entire time it takes to pay off the loan.)

PAYMENT	DATE DUE	INTEREST	PRINCIPAL	MO. PMT.
1	01/10/85	$844.00	$ 28.00	$872.00
2	02/10/85	$843.00	$ 29.00	$872.00
3	03/10/85	$842.00	$ 30.00	$872.00
180	12/10/99	$436.00	$436.00	$872.00
360	12/10/14	$ 22.00	$850.00	$872.00

As the amortization schedule shows, the monthly payment of $872 is made up of two parts which, in the first month, is $844 of INTEREST MONEY TOTALLY FOR THE BANK and only $28 of PRINCIPAL, which reduces the amount you owe on the loan. By the end of the first year, this mortgage will have paid $10,101.25 to the BANKERS on interest, or profit for them, and only $365.75 of the total amount you paid was applied toward the principal to reduce the loan. As a result, although you will pay $10,467 during the first year on this $88,000 loan (12 payments of $872 each) at the end of the first year you will still owe $87,634.25 on the loan!!!!

By the time the home mortgage is amortized (completely paid off by the monthly payments), how much principal will have been paid back to the bank? The answer is of course—$88,000—-the amount originally borrowed. But how much interest will have been paid to the banker? The answer is $225,920! For this $88,000 home, the borrower (you) will end up paying a total of $313,920!! In other words, you will have "bought" this home FOUR TIMES!! A TOTAL OF 72% (Almost three-fourths) OF ALL YOUR MONTHLY PAYMENTS WILL HAVE GONE TO THE BANKER AS INTEREST! Most homeowners are totally unaware of these startling facts! It's not hard to pay off your house once. It only becomes difficult when you are asked to pay it off three or four times in interest.

However, you can avoid this situation by making early principal payments. Your goal should be to pay off the principal (the amount you actually owe) as soon as possible. To make an early principal payment means to pay the principal amounts ahead of the time table shown on your amortization schedule. Making early principal payments eliminates all further interest on the amount of principal paid. You will not be charged the interest you would have paid had you paid the principal according to the schedule.

Making early principal payments is very simple. All you do is write a second check which you include with your monthly mortgage check. Write "early principal payment" on the second check on the line in the lower left corner. Any early principal payment is treated by the bank as a direct reduction of the remaining principal on your loan. That means it reduces the amount you actually owe on your loan. The interest which you would have paid on that principal had you paid it according to the payment schedule rather than making extra principal payments, will be eliminated by the bank from its records. In other words YOU WILL NOT HAVE TO PAY THE INTEREST and that is really good stewardship of God's blessings.

There are no restrictions against early principal payments. It is completely legal. You can make early principal payments in any amount. Some banks prefer that you make early principal payments in certain amounts, such as $25.00. Others have no restrictions. Call the loan officer at your bank and ask him how they would prefer your early principal payment to be made. Remember, your early principal payment must be made in addition to your normal monthly payment.

Many years ago when I was still deeply in debt, the Lord spoke to me one night while I was praying. He said, "Do you remember how easy it was to get into the fix you are in now? You spent $29.00 here, $19.00 there, $106.00 over here, and so on, and so every month, almost without realizing it, you went deeper into debt. Well, you must follow the identical process to get out of debt. If you will make early principal payments of $29.00 one month, $19.00 another month, $106.00 another month, and so on each and every month, soon you will begin to see your debts decrease just like you originally saw them increase."

The amazing truth which God revealed to me is that the pathway out of debt is like retracing the steps taken in walking into debt. Just as small sums were spent which over a period of time added up to a large debt, even the smallest principal payments will, over a period of time, eliminate that debt and save you thousands of dollars in interest.

You can obtain amortization schedules for your loan by calling your bank and requesting one. They can be obtained from loan companies, computer companies and banks.

Incidentally, this principle will work on your VISA payment, your car payment, and on any other loan you may make. Make early principal payments and walk free of debt.

Chapter 7

THE STOREHOUSE

God wants you to have a storehouse or a savings account which you add to faithfully. And He wants to bless your storehouse.

In this chapter we are going to deal with the storehouse. A storehouse is essential to you. A storehouse can help you *get out* of debt. A storehouse can help you *stay out* of debt. A storehouse is surplus provision. It is extra money over and above what you need to live on and pay your bills. In modern English we call the storehouse a savings account.

Deuteronomy 28:8 says, "The Lord shall command the blessing upon thee in thy storehouses, and in all that thou settest thine hand unto; and he shall bless thee in the land which the Lord thy God giveth thee." God wants to bless your storehouse or your savings account! Obviously, He can't bless your storehouse if you don't have one!

You may be thinking, "Deuteronomy is an Old Testament book. How can I be sure that scripture applies to me?" Look at Galatians 3:13,14: "Christ hath redeemed us from the curse of the law, being made a curse for us: for it is written, cursed is everyone that hangeth on a tree: That the blessing of Abraham might come on the Gentiles through Jesus Christ." These verses tell us that Christ redeemed us or brought us out from under the curse of the law by becoming a curse Himself so that the blessings of Abraham could come upon us.

The curse of the law is the consequences which come upon people who disobey the laws of God. Those consequences are listed in Deuteronomy 28:15-68. Also listed in Deuteronomy 28:1-14, are the blessings which come upon people who obey the laws of God. According to Galatians 3:13, 14, one of the things Christ did for us by going to the Cross was to free us from the curse of the law and open the door to the blessings listed in Deuteronomy 28. Deuteronomy 28 most certainly applies to us today.

You see, the blessings listed in Deuteronomy 28 which God promised to Abraham and his descendants belong to us too!

Galations 3:29 says, "And if ye be Christ's then are ye Abraham's seed, and heirs according to the promise." Because we are Christ's, we have become the seed of Abraham. That means we are his descendants, his heirs. Galations 3:7 says, "Know ye therefore that they which are of faith, the same are the children of Abraham." We are children of Abraham because we have faith in Christ. As Abraham's heirs, *WE* are entitled to all the blessings promised to him and his children under the Old Covenant. Remember also what we pointed out in Chapter 2: that the New Covenant includes the benefits of the Old Covenant and more. If a blessed storehouse was part of the Old Covenant—and it was—then New Covenant believers have the right to a blessed storehouse.

Over the years as God led me first from the Land of Lack to the Land of Even, and then into the Land of Prosperity, He has taught me about two types of storehouses or barns—big barns and little barns. If you look closely at Deuteronomy 28:8 you will see that God wants to bless your storehouses (plural). That means more than one! Let's take a moment to look at each type.

A big barn is a savings account. I'm not talking about an account with millions of dollars in it which you never touch. Matthew 6:19 says, "Lay not up for yourselves treasures upon earth, where moth and rust doth corrupt." Something which is moth eaten and rusted isn't used much. I'm not talking about an account in which you save for a rainy day. If you save for a rainy day, you'll get one!

I'm talking about an account with enough money in it that you never have to go back into lack. For example, suppose you need a new refrigerator or some other household item. You can go to your storehouse or savings account and get the money instead of going to Household Finance. Or, suppose a guest minister comes to your church to speak and you purpose in your heart to give a special offering to his ministry. You can get the money from your storehouse! A storehouse keeps you prepared for any unexpected expense or expenditure which might come along.

How large should your big barn or savings account be? The Bible gives us some guidelines. In Genesis 41, Joseph, a descendant of Abraham, interpreted some dreams which Pharoah of Egypt had. According to Joseph the dreams were from God and told of seven years of plenty followed by seven years of famine just ahead. Because Joseph interpreted the dreams, Pharoah placed Joseph in charge of preparing for what was to come.

God gave Joseph a plan of preparation. Genesis 41:34 tells us that Joseph had a fifth of the produce of the land gathered up and stored during the years of plenty to provide food for the years of famine. Joseph's storehouse was one fifth of the entire production of the land. Joseph stored twenty percent of his income. Since the idea to store one fifth came from God, I believe we can use it as a guideline for ourselves. Our storehouse should be filled with twenty percent of our income.

That may seem like an impossible amount to put into a savings account. You may be thinking, "After I tithe, give an offering, and send to Brother Hagin and Brother Copeland, and pay my bills, too, I'm supposed to put twenty percent in savings? There's no way!" Yes there is! It takes a decision to do it, determination to accomplish it, and discipline to get the money together, put it in an account and not take it out. And it can be done if you decide to do it.

I want to mention an important point here. DO NOT LEAN ON YOUR STOREHOUSE. LEAN ON GOD! He is your provider, your source of supply. If you find yourself relying on the storehouse rather than on God, clear it out! You are not to store up treasure on earth! You are not to trust in uncertain riches! You are to apply principles of godly wisdom and good stewardship so that God can bless your storehouse with more and you can be ready to distribute and willing to communicate (I Timothy 6:18).

My family and I also use little storehouses or barns. Our little barns are actually envelopes which we use to store money for specific purposes. Let's say we have a large car insurance bill which comes due in March and September. We take an envelope and write "car insurance" on it. Every week between March and September we put a certain amount of money into that envelope. Once that money is put into the envelope we do not take it out no matter what. The envelope is almost like a little escrow account. When the September bill arrives we take the money we've been putting into the envelope each week and mail it off with the balance of the payment. By saving money in our little barn each week, we don't have to use a large chunk of our income when the bill arrives. We already have the money in our little storehouse. You can use this system with any type of bill—utilities, car payment, house payment, etc.

God watches what you do with your money. If He sees that you handle it well and in line with principles from His Word, He'll bless you with more. As we read in Deuteronomy 28:8, God desires to bless your storehouse. Proverbs 3:9, 10 says, "Honour the Lord with thy substance, and with the first fruits of all thine increase: so shall thy barns be filled with plenty, and thy presses shall burst out with new wine." To honor the Lord with your first fruits means to tithe. As we saw in Chapter 4, tithing is a Biblical principle which God can use to bless you. There are certain rewards connected to cooperating with that principle. Proverbs 3:10 says that one of the results of tithing is that your barns or storehouses or savings accounts shall be filled with plenty. God wants to bless you financially, so begin cooperating with Him. Tithe! Open a storehouse! It is God's will that you have storehouses and that they be filled with plenty! If you don't have a storehouse, open one today.

Chapter 8

THE BIBLE WAY TO MAKE IT THROUGH THE WINTER

One reason people end up in debt is because they have trouble making it through the winter. Winter means higher utility bills. For seasonal workers it can mean layoffs. But, the Bible has some practical instructions on how to make it through the winter without suffering financially. You need to learn these simple tips if you are going to get out and stay out of debt. There should be no lack in the Body of Christ—not in the summer or the winter. Philippians 4:19 says that it is God's will to meet all of our needs according to His riches in glory. If we can learn to prepare for winter, winter will be the easiest time financially instead of the toughest time.

Proverbs 10:5 says, "He that gathereth in summer is a wise son: but he that sleepeth in harvest is a son that causeth shame." Summer is the time to gather or prepare according to this verse. Now this verse is talking about the literal summer—June, July, and August. But, let me take a moment to point out that there is a summertime in your life—the days of your youth. And you should use those days to prepare for the winter of your life—old age.

There are certain things you should do in the natural while

you are young such as buy a house. But there are certain things you need to do in the spirit too. Ecclesiastes 12:1 says, "Remember now thy Creator in the days of thy youth, while the evil days come not, nor the years draw nigh." Youth is the time to fill yourself with healing scriptures so that when arthritis and other "old age" diseases try to attack your body, you'll be prepared to fight them off! You should prepare in your youth so that you can be as vigorous at 70 as you are at 40. Youth is the time to strengthen yourself with scriptures promising that God will meet all of your financial needs so that when you reach the age of "fixed income" you'll know that there is no such thing as a fixed income for a child of God.

Now, let's consider the literal summer and winter. Proverbs 10:5 tells us that a wise person prepares or gathers in the summertime. But a shameful son sleeps during harvest time. What is harvest time? It is the time to work and gather in supplies in preparation for winter. You can and you should prepare for winter during the summer and harvest time.

How can you prepare if you aren't a farmer who can actually go out to the fields and literally gather in food? It's very simple. In early summer get an envelope and mark it HEAT BILL. Then, every week of the summer put money in that envelope—$10, $15, $20—whatever you can manage! People have more money in the summer because expenses drop for most families. Take some of the extra money and make an extra car payment or two. That way when the high utility bills come in during the winter, you can skip a car payment because you are paid ahead! Christianity is so practical!

You may be thinking, "I could never get the money together for an extra car payment or bills six months in the future." You're right, you can't UNLESS YOU MAKE THE DECISION TO DO IT. Then you must discipline yourself and use good judgment. Don't take the extra money you've got due to lower summer utilities and run out and buy a new dress or a pair of shoes. Obey the Bible and gather or prepare for winter in the summer.

Actually, it boils down to good stewardship or wisely using the things which God has given you. The Bible has much to say about good stewardship. The basic Bible principle of stewardship is that he who handles his money, his abilities, his talents, and his time wisely will be given even more. And just as importantly, he who does not will lose even what he has (Matthew 25:14-30). Learn to handle your affairs wisely.

In Genesis 41 we see this principle of preparation again. Pharaoh had two dreams which disturbed him greatly. Pharaoh sent for Joseph who was able to interpret the dreams. Joseph said the dreams of Pharaoh were from God and that the dreams showed there would be seven years of plenty in the land followed by seven years of famine (verses 25-31). Joseph further said that Pharaoh should select a man to supervise preparation of the land for the seven lean years during the seven years of plenty.

Joseph was put in charge of that task. As the story continues on in the rest of the chapter, we see that under the leadership of Joseph, one-fifth of all the provision of the land was laid up in storehouses during the years of great blessing. The result was that during the years of famine, the Egyptians had plenty to eat as well as enough to share with other countries. Once again, we see the principle of preparing for lean times during the times of plenty.

Let me make an important point here. When I talk about putting aside money for the future, I'm not talking about saving for a rainy day or an operation. If you save for a rainy day, you'll get a rainy day. If you save for an operation, you'll have one. I'm talking about putting Biblical principles of wisdom into practice. God told Joseph to store up food. Because of His foreknowledge, God knew that some bad times were ahead and He wanted Joseph prepared. Because Joseph followed the wisdom and direction of God, the bad times were not bad for him at all! They were actually good times because Joseph was prepared for them. When you store up things in summer, you are not expecting and preparing to experience evil in winter, you are preparing to breeze through rough times because you are following the wisdom of God.

Let's look at Proverbs 6:6-8. "Go to the ant, thou sluggard; consider her ways, and be wise: which having no guide, overseer, or ruler, provideth her meat in summer, and gathereth her food in the harvest." The Bible tells us to consider or look at the ant. We can learn about how to make it through the winter by looking at the ant. How does the ant prepare for winter? The ant WORKS HARD ALL SUMMER GATHERING AND STORING food for the winter. The Holy Spirit did not mention the ant in this verse simply to fill up space. We can learn some things by observing the activities of the ant.

The ants work in harmony. A family can work as a team to store up for winter. Make it a family project to get together some extra car payments or something similar. The ants have no overseer to force them to work. They simply do it! It's the same with us. God won't force you to be wise and prepare for winter. You have to make the decision to do it and then follow through with it! The ants are faithful and consistent in their work. We need those qualities too, in order to prepare for winter. If you save money in June, then blow it in July, you won't be prepared for winter.

Proverbs 30:25 says, "The ants are a people not strong, yet they prepare their meat in the summer." The ants may not be strong; they may not be mighty. Yet what do they do? They prepare. They prepare their meat in summer. Remember Proverbs 6:6 told us to consider or take note of the ways of the ant. What does the ant do? The ant prepares in summer. We need to do so as well.

We can learn a lot about how to make it through the winter without any lack by observing the ants and their activities.

Proverbs 2:7 says, "He layeth up sound wisdom for the righteous." God has put this principle of preparing in the summer into His Word so that we can act on it and benefit from it. And Proverbs 2:6 says, "For the Lord giveth wisdom." He'll give you specific instructions about how you can gather in the summer in your own personal life. He'll show you ways to save. Just pray and ask Him to show you where you need to make some adjustments. Then, He'll make you a wise son by showing you where, how and what to gather in the summer to help you make it through the winter.

One Final Word

It is possible to get out of debt. If you follow the principles laid out in this book, you can move from the Land of Lack to the Land of Even and right on into the Land of Prosperity. God is not a respecter of persons. What He did for my family and me, He will do for you too.

APPENDIX

Confidential List of Household and Family Expenses

For: _____   Date: _____

	Monthly	Annual	Changes
Food/Groceries, Allowances, etc.			
House Payment			
Approximate property taxes and insurance			
Clothes			
Utilities			
Telephone			
Cleaners			
New household purchases			
Auto expenses -- Gas, oil, tires, repairs			
Entertainment			
Club dues			
Vacation trips, camps, etc.			
Miscellaneous -- horses, boats, airplanes, etc.			
Music, dancing, and other lessons			
Personal life insurance - husband			
Personal life insurance - wife			
Hospitalization insurance			
Disability insurance			
Professional liability insurance			
Insurance on cars, boats, jewelry, etc.			
Homeowner's insurance (if separate from mortgage pmt.)			
Inside household help			
Household maintenance and repairs			
Yard and outside maintenance help			
Pool maintenance, if any			
Donations to church, charities, etc.			
Subscriptions			
Medical expenses (doctor, dentist, prescriptions)			
Gifts			
Personal expenses for family			
Unreimbursed business expenses			
Other expenses			
Total Estimated Household and Family Expenses			

Debt Repayment Priority

Lendor	Outstanding Balance	Annual Interest Rate	Monthly Payment	Repayment Priority

Monthly Storehouse

JAN	FEB	MAR	APR	MAY	JUN	JUL	AUG	SEP	OCT	NOV	DEC
$	$	$	$	$	$	$	$	$	$	$	$

Deuteronomy 28:8
"The Lord shall command the blessing upon thee in thy storehouses, and in all that thou settest thine hand unto; and he shall bless thee in the land which the Lord thy God giveth thee."

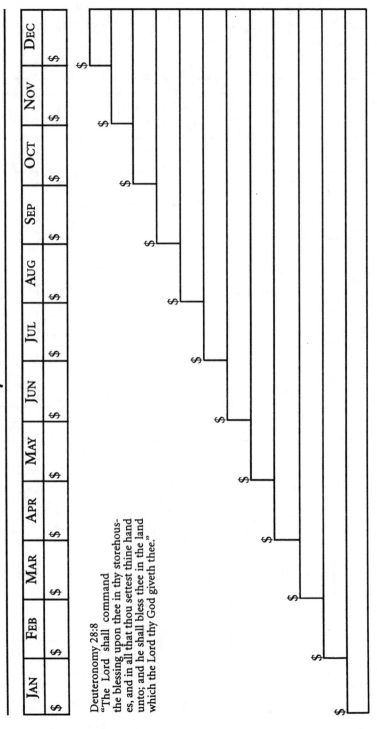

Road Map to Prosperity

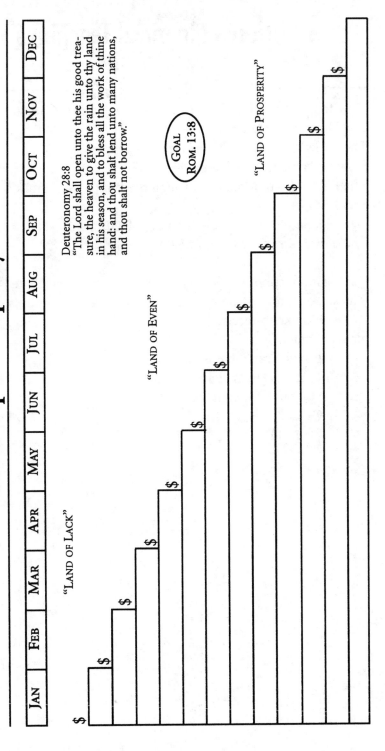

JAN	FEB	MAR	APR	MAY	JUN	JUL	AUG	SEP	OCT	NOV	DEC

"LAND OF LACK"

"LAND OF EVEN"

"LAND OF PROSPERITY"

Deuteronomy 28:8
"The Lord shall open unto thee his good treasure, the heaven to give the rain unto thy land in his season, and to bless all the work of thine hand: and thou shalt lend unto many nations, and thou shalt not borrow."

GOAL
ROM. 13:8

Additional Financial Teachings
by David Crank

How to Open the Windows of Heaven — 4 tapes / $16.00
The Hundred Fold Return — 3 tapes / $12.00
The Bible Way to Get Out of Debt — 2 tapes / $8.00
How To Pay Off Your Home — 6 tapes / $24.00
The Bible Way to Make It Through the Winter — 2 tapes / $8.00
New Revelation in Tithe — 2 tapes / $8.00
The Storehouse — 2 tapes / $8.00

David Crank conducts financial seminars across the United States. For information concerning a seminar in your area or if you would like to receive a complete teaching tape catalog, please contact:

> David Crank Ministries
> 1416 Larkin Williams Road
> St. Louis, Missouri 63026
> Or Call:
> (314) 343-4359

Notes

Notes

Notes

Notes

Notes

Notes